MW01043723

When it's *YOU* Against *THEM*:

Keeping a Positive Attitude Despite It All

Kathy A. Eubanks

VG Publishing. Chesterfield, Michigan

1

When It's YOU Against THEM:

Keeping a Positive Attitude Despite It All

Table of Contents

About the Author
Acknowledgments
Warning-Disclaimer

Chapter	Title	Page
One	Why Live It Up?	9
Two	Wake Up	17
Three	Link Up	25
Four	Speak Up	41
Five	Lighten Up	53
Six	Listen Up	61
Seven	Change Up	73
Eight	Lift Up	77
Nine	Charge Up	83
Ten	Reach Up	91
Eleven	Never, Ever Give Up	95
Twelve	Keep It Up	101
References		117

About The Author

Kathy Eubanks is currently director of training for Voyager Group, LLC, a company that delivers  cutting-edge leadership and motivational training. She has a passion for educating people and giving them tools to find their greatest potential and joy from life. Kathy has 20 years of experience educating adults who are aiming to improve their opportunities. Her students have included college students, physicians, business owners and CEO's.

KATHY A. EUBANKS
Voyager Group, LLC
www.KathyEubanks.com
51613 Sass Road
Chesterfield, MI 48047
Email: *info@voyagergroupllc.com*
586-598-0268

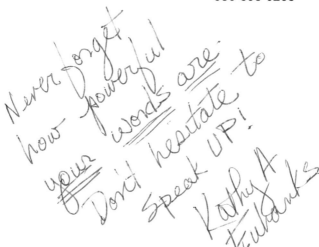

5

ACKNOWLEDGMENTS

I would like to sincerely thank all of those people who have helped me put this book together. It would be very difficult to name all of my friends and colleagues who have supported and encouraged me along the way. You know who you are; I can't thank you enough.

I would especially like to thank my family, John, Jacky and Kylee. You inspire me and bring out the best in me every day. I would also like to thank my parents (Joan & Chet), brothers, sister, in-laws, aunts, uncles, cousins, nephews, and nieces. A special thank you to Aunt Virge and Diane. Aunt Virge, you always told me I could do it. Diane, here is your idea in print.

Warning-Disclaimer

This book is designed to provide information on strategies for maintaining a positive attitude. It is sold with the understanding that the publisher and author are not engaged in rendering legal, accounting or other professional services. If legal or other expert assistance is required, the services of a competent professional should be sought.

It is not the purpose of this manual to reprint all the information that is otherwise available to authors and/or publishers, but instead to complement, amplify and supplement other texts. You are urged to read all the available material, learn as much as possible and tailor the information to your individual needs. For more information, see the resources listed in the References.

Every effort has been made to make this book as complete and accurate as possible. However, there may be mistakes, both typographical and in content. Therefore, this text should be used only as a general guide and not as the ultimate source for maintaining a positive attitude. Furthermore, this book contains information that is current only up to the printing date.

The purpose of this book is to educate and entertain. The author and VG Publishing shall have neither liability nor responsibility to any person or entity with respect to any loss or damage caused, or alleged to have been cause, directly or indirectly, by the information contained in this book.

If you do not wish to be bound by the above, you may return this book to the publisher for a full refund.

Chapter 1
WHY STAY POSITIVE?

Why do we need to stay positive? Everything and everyone else is so negative. Just turn on a local or national news broadcast. The headlines of any paper scream tragedy, crisis and despair. Attend a family or community function and hear all of the latest gossip or listen to others reiterate their health and personal problems. Why should WE bother; why should WE stay upbeat when clearly no one else is.

REASONS FOR STAYING POSITIVE.

- Attitudes are contagious. If you are enjoying what you are doing, chances are that other people will catch that enthusiasm. As a professor, I taught science classes: biology, natural science, and anatomy & physiology. I loved science; I still do. One of the reasons has to do with some of the science teachers I had in elementary and high school. They really enjoyed teaching science and communicated their love for the topic.

- Life is just a lot more fun with a positive attitude! Not that everything we do is fun but if you are going to have to get up every morning *and* raise a family *and* commute to work *and* clean your home *and* whatever thousand other things you need to do to survive, why not enjoy it? Or at least enjoy it more. When you are having fun and enjoying life, everyone around you benefits.

- If you are in a position of authority or influence, maintaining a positive, can-do attitude is essential to your success. Think of the last project you worked on. Did the leadership have a positive or a negative attitude about it? If the leadership was excited about the project, there was a much greater probability the project would be successful. If not, everyone involved or impacted by the project would sense it, and the chances of success were greatly reduced.

- Our health is also affected by our attitudes. There is a great deal of evidence, both scientific and anecdotal, to support this. Entire books have been written about this topic alone. However, the bottom line is that a positive attitude makes you less likely to get sick and also improves your body's ability to heal and recover when it is ill.

If you still find yourself skeptical, you may want to try an experiment that I observed. I attended a workshop in which the facilitator demonstrated this connection in a simple way. One participant was asked to join the facilitator up front. The facilitator had the participant push up on her arm while she applied a continuous amount of downward pressure. The participant was asked to recall in great detail different experiences.

The rest of us watched how the recollection of these events affected her strength. When she was recalling positive experiences, she had no trouble raising her arm against the resistance. When she recalled negative experiences of shame, sadness, guilt and grief, she could barely hold her own against the applied force. This experiment illustrated in a very simple way how attitude affects us physically. Find a partner and try it yourself.

- If improving your own health is not enough reason for improving your attitude, there is another compelling reason: The 'world' in which future generations live, will be shaped by our attitudes. Whether we like it or not, our attitudes will not only influence the attitudes of our children and grandchildren, it will also shape the world in which they live. This imparts on us an awesome responsibility.

  Those of us that have any contact with children-- parents, teachers, coaches, scout leaders, aunts, uncles, cousins, step parents--have an especially important responsibility. A wise person once said, **"More is caught than is taught!"** Children will pick up our positive or negative attitudes. Their view of the world will ultimately be shaped by this. Wow, if that doesn't make a person stop and think!

Even people who do not have direct contact with future generations have an indirect impact. We all come in contact with other adults. We impact the worlds of adults who do influence children. The old saying says, *"If Mama ain't happy, then no one is happy."* If mom or dad spends 40-60 hours a week in a very negative work environment, it is likely to affect what happens at home. Most of us can't just shut off the frustrations we experience at work when we walk in the front door of our homes. Whether you work with children or not, each of us either directly or indirectly impacts the future.

WHAT CAN I DO?

- The good thing is that being more positive is something people can develop. You don't have to be born happy or be raised with a Pollyanna childhood. Just like we can develop better habits in terms of our health, we can develop habits that will help us be more positive.

- As you start working on a few of the suggestions in this book, you will notice how it becomes easier each day. Research indicates that it takes 21 days of repetition to develop a new habit. It will take 21 days to make affirmations a part of your morning routine. Changing your outlook on life takes longer; it is a process that requires us to implement the habits over a lifetime. Just as establishing a healthy diet is ongoing, so is establishing a healthy attitude.

CAUTION.

- The ideas in this book are not to replace medical intervention for those suffering severe depression or other mental health afflictions. There are times when medical and psychological therapies are invaluable. These ideas can be used in conjunction with other therapies for the total well-being of the individual.

HOW TO USE THIS BOOK.

- Although presented sequentially, individuals don't have to implement the strategies contained in this book in any particular order. The strategies are designed to build on each other. Select a few to implement right away.

- When they become more of a habit and easier to do, go ahead and add a few more. You will see the effects on your life and will want to try more and more strategies to maintain your positive lifestyle.

- Eventually, you will begin to notice changes in the way you feel. You will start generating results and this will lead to more positive-ness in your life. In anatomy classes, we used to refer to this as a positive feedback loop. One success leads to more and more successes.

- I can't wait to hear back from you and about how you are leading a more positive life!

Chapter 2
WAKE UP

We are responsible for our own happiness.

Before you can begin to do the rest of the things suggested in this book, you have to wake up and realize that no other person can make you happy. The responsibility for your own happiness rests squarely on your shoulders. Too many of us spend our time waiting for someone or something to make us happy.

A recent experience I had illustrates this point.

My husband, John, and I decided to take advantage of the lower interest rates and decided to refinance our home mortgage. As part of the process, we needed to have our home appraised. As with most appointments, this needed to be scheduled during the day which was not too much of a problem for me since I have a home office. When the appraiser saw my office, she inquired about the type of work that I perform. I happily explained that I provide leadership and motivational training.

She replied with a smile and, "Hmph," and continued with her inspection. This remark was followed by silence. I tried to interpret what her response meant.

When we returned to the kitchen a few minutes later, she inquired, "Isn't that an impossible task? You can't truly motivate anyone other than yourself. Doesn't that have to come from within?"

She was right, that truly does come from within. I explained how I share with leaders how important it is to maintain a positive attitude in order to keep their teams and colleagues motivated. I also explained how in motivational training, I give people tools that they can utilize to improve attitude but it ultimately is an individual's own responsibility.

I then shared with her some of the ideas I share in training. She concurred that these were some of the same things that she utilized to stay positive. She also talked about the implications for her in terms of being self employed. She shared how these same actions have influenced her high school aged son.

So often I run into people who are waiting for the right conditions to improve their mood and attitude. "When I meet that special person..." or "when I have enough money..." or "when I buy that..." or "when I get that job...." All are waiting for some outside influence to make a difference for them; they relinquish their control over their own happiness to something or someone else.

Sometimes people relinquish that control in more subtle ways. One of my favorite statements is, "I can't wait until I am on vacation...." As if to say that one can be miserable for 50 weeks out of a year and then try to cram all of the joy into two weeks. It is not okay to inflict a miserable attitude on your family and co-workers for 50 weeks and expect to make it all up to your family in two short weeks. That includes the people you work with who are glad to have you out of the office for two weeks!

WHY TAKE CONTROL OF OUR ATTITUDE?

- When we take back the control for our own personal happiness, this frees us from having those people around us dictating our attitude. When we recognize that we are solely responsible for our attitude, we don't allow others to suck us into their bad attitudes. It gives us the freedom to say to a moody teenager, spouse or co-worker, "You can choose to be in a foul mood today, but I am not going to let it bring me down." We can sympathize with others who are negative without being brought down ourselves.

- It also gives us the ability to choose, each day, what type of attitude we are going to have. We can start out each day, saying to ourselves: "I am choosing to have a good attitude today." It astounds me still to see how differently people respond to events, situations and people when they have consciously decided to have a good attitude.

- We become much less reactive. Have you ever noticed how you respond differently to minor (and some times not so minor) inconveniences that come your way? When you have a bad attitude, it seems like everything and everyone is out to get you. You lock your keys in your car, get cut off by another driver, get delayed in traffic and you feel like everything is working against you. It feels like

21

Murphy's Law, "What can go wrong will go wrong," is at work

- When we are approaching life with a negative attitude we become much more reactive and less proactive.

Those same incidences, traffic, locked keys and rude drivers, take on a whole different perspective when we have a good attitude. They become inconveniences as opposed to insurmountable tasks. We suddenly find an alternative route to get out of the traffic. We remember where the spare keys are. Instead of getting irate at the other driver, we give the abrupt driver some slack by assuming he was in a real hurry to get somewhere.

WHY DO SOME PEOPLE REMAIN NEGATIVE?

Despite knowing this, many people still choose to be negative. There are certain psychological pay offs for remaining negative. Negative people may perceive that they are getting more attention in the form of sympathy despite the fact that evidence indicates just the opposite.

People with a negative attitude need to understand the rewards for having a positive outlook. They need to know that the benefits far outweigh those of having a negative attitude. From a purely health perspective, they need to recognize the affects of their choice to remain negative.

If you are someone who continues to have a bad attitude despite the fact that you know intellectually that it is more advantageous to have a positive attitude, take some time to examine why you are continuing down this path. Identify what benefits you truly obtain from maintaining a bad attitude. Weigh that up against the benefits of a positive attitude. Then choose. Just choose either to have a positive or negative attitude. Make a decision and follow through on it.

Chapter 3
LINK UP

We become like the people we spend the most time with.

I grew up in with my three brothers and sister in a small three bedroom ranch in Detroit. We had one telephone in our home. That phone was in the kitchen. If any of us were having a phone conversation with our friends, privacy was virtually impossible. Mom or dad (or worse a younger sibling) was always around to overhear at least one half of the conversation. When I was a teenager, this was horrible. I can remember stretching the cord to its absolute maximum and sitting on the floor in another room whispering into the telephone the details of crushes and gossip, all of this while mom was cooking dinner. My parents always had a handle on which friend we were talking to and the topics of our conversations. Can you believe their nerve! I was really convinced that I had the worst parents in the world.

The bottom line was that my parents knew who I was spending time with. Not only did they know the kids, they knew their parents. They knew what school they went to and what mass they attended on Sunday. If someone had a reputation, either good or bad, they knew it. If we started hanging out with troublemakers, mom and dad knew right away. In their vast experience (which I completely dismissed as a teenager) they knew that *we become like the people we spend the most time with.*

Understanding this point is crucial to developing a positive attitude. If we become like the people we spend the most time with, we need to make sure we are surrounding ourselves with positive, uplifting, life giving people.

When I was teaching, I can remember having conversations in the central office of the biology department with other professors. The conversations often centered on complaints about lack of supplies, not enough lab equipment, having to share office space, poor support staff, and most often about how horrible the students were. It is really pathetic to think of how these profs viewed the students who they were teaching. I am sure the students sensed the professors true feelings in the classroom. These 'horrible' students were our reason for being there.

With the encouragement of my dean, I became involved with some of the advanced educational opportunities offered to the professors. I was put on committees with the 'best of the best' of the college. I was working side by side with profs who loved their jobs and their students. Conversations centered on the possibilities as opposed to the limitations. It was an incredible learning experience for me. These were people who were always striving for excellence despite being surrounded by people who disdained their actions. These profs formed their own informal support network. We were from all different disciplines: psychology, literature, art, accounting, criminal justice, and biology to name a few. I was even invited into their classrooms to observe their teaching styles and learn from them. I am so grateful to my dean for steering me in the right direction when she sensed my frustration with the majority of my colleagues in the science department.

As a result of these associations, my teaching improved dramatically. We were using teaching methods in science classes that were normally used only in the arts. These methods were closely evaluated and very successful at promoting critical thinking skills. I was able to report my findings in papers; I was invited to co-author a laboratory manual. My retention rates were very high. In 1996, I was awarded the *Excellence in Teaching* award.

The most important thing, however, were the benefits to my students. They continually exceeded my expectations; every semester I set the bar higher. My dean and colleagues would come in to observe student presentations and other activities that were taking place within my classes. One colleague, whom I highly respected, popped in to my classroom very close to the end of the semester. He was shocked to find a full classroom of highly energized and motivated students working on team projects. These were things that just normally didn't happen at a community college.

I am sure most of us can share stories similar to these. They do not always involve our work environment. It may involve acquaintances or even family members. We can share stories of striking up a conversation with someone at work, or a social gathering, and how, at the end of the encounter, we felt drained.

It happened to me once in the dentist's office. I made an innocent comment on the weather to a person in the waiting room. Before I knew what happened, this person had shared every health problem, family and marital problem that she had. I was relieved to get into the dentist's chair for a root canal!

The people we associate with are especially important when we hold a position of leadership. Surrounding ourselves with positive, make-a-way people rubs off on us. We will rise up (or sink down) to the people around us. Attitude is contagious. Outstanding leaders will surround themselves with winners and other outstanding leaders.

WHAT CAN YOU DO WHEN YOU ARE SURROUNDED BY NEGATIVE PEOPLE?

So what do you do when you know you have to be around negative people? There are times when we HAVE to be with such people. It might be family members; it might be coworkers or colleagues, but there are times when we don't have a great deal of choice about who we are with. What do we do then?

- If we know ahead of time that we are going to be with negative people, prepare yourself. I personally use prayer and music. When I am on my way to places where I know I am going to be surrounded by negativity, I say a quick prayer for protection. Then I listen to my favorite music on the way to the event. I make sure it is upbeat, happy music; often it is inspirational. It is usually music that makes me want to get up and dance. If I am alone in my car, the volume is turned up and I am singing along as if I was in concert. I know I am not the best singer, but who cares? It makes me feel good. Chances are, my fingers will be tapping the rhythm out on the steering wheel and I may be bopping my head from side to side as well.

- A colleague of mine prays for the Holy Spirit to place a shield in front of her to protect her from negativity.

She visualizes the 'bad' bouncing right off her shield.

- Another colleague pictures herself surrounded by a bubble. This bubble is pervious to compliments and positive feelings and impervious to negativity. The good stuff gets through and the bad stays outside the bubble.

- Other people visualize the negative comments and attitudes as rolling right off of their back.

- Prior to the encounters, visualize yourself protected by a bubble or shield. Imagine pouring a slick, oily liquid over your head. Smell it; taste it; feel it coating your body, picture in your mind negative comments sliding off your body.

- As a kid we had a rhyme we would say when being harassed by other children. "I am rubber; you are glue. Whatever you say bounces off of me and sticks to you." Repeating these words to a bully usually didn't give me much comfort. However, as adults we can use this rhyme more effectively. We can repeat the rhyme in our mind and visualize the negative comments bouncing off of us.

REMOVE YOURSELF FROM A NEGATIVE ENVIRONMENT.

In some cases, you may need to actually remove yourself from the negative environment. This may also require you to insulate yourself until you are able to get out of the negativity.

Several years ago, my husband worked in an environment that was very negative and also had a value system very different from ours. When he realized that in order to be successful in this corporation, he was going to have to compromise his integrity, he made the decision to find a new job. This search took quite a bit of time. During that interim he did some things to shelter himself from the environment.

INTERIM STRATEGIES.

- First, he decided to eat lunch outside of the office every day. His lunch hour was usually spent in a library, bookstore or at a park (weather permitting).

- He did not socialize with the people who did not share our values. He sought out people in the office who did share his values and spent time with them. These strategies served him well while searching for a new job.

- Decisive ignorance can be another strategy. I co-facilitated a training session for middle management for a very large corporation. I was so enthusiastic about the training material, that I assumed everyone attending the training program would be equally enthusiastic. It never crossed my mind that the manager's would be resistant to the program.

During the morning session, the managers repeatedly challenged the material. I assumed that they were challenging us because they already had an excellent working knowledge of the material. I assumed that they were trying to just obtain a greater depth of knowledge and better understanding of the application of the material.

At lunch two of the managers confessed that prior to commencement of the program, all of the managers attending conspired to sabotage the training. They all agreed to sandbag our program by stalling and asking irrelevant questions. Despite their best efforts, the two managers told us, they were not able to succeed. In this case, our decisive ignorance worked to our advantage.

DEVELOP A CORE GROUP OF FRIENDS AND ADVISORS.

This core group is made up of our advisors, friends and mentors. It is composed of individuals of whom we can seek advice from and be confident that they have our best interest in mind. They are people who tend to build others up. Avoid those who habitually criticize and find fault with people and organizations. Such are the key things to look for when putting together your core group. These traits are more important than career, economic status, social standing, etc.

WHO SHOULD WE SPEND TIME WITH?

Since we have now determined that we need to surround ourselves with positive people, we need to take some time to assess the overall attitude of those people we spend the most time with. On the following page, list the people that you spend the most time with.

LINK UP ASSESSMENT
Make a list of the people that you spend the most time with.

Name	+1,-1, 0
1. _____	_____
2. _____	_____
3. _____	_____
4. _____	_____
5. _____	_____
6. _____	_____
7. _____	_____
8. _____	_____

Rate each person's overall attitude.

+1 = Overall Positive Attitude
-1 = Overall Negative Attitude
0 = Neutral

Examine your overall results for this exercise.

After listing the people you spend the most time with, quickly go back and rate the overall attitude of each person. Give the person a '+1' if they have an overall attitude that is positive. If you walk away from a meeting with this person and you generally feel better, give that person a '+1'. If the opposite is true, rate the person a '-1'. When you walk away from this person and you feel drained, that person gets a '-1'. If your dealings with someone are generally neither positive or negative, rate the person as neutral, '0'. People with a neutral rating often include business/work colleagues or customers in which you exchange information without any real emotional interaction. This could also apply to those people whose general moods vary greatly. They are either in a great mood or a rotten mood.

WHAT ARE YOUR RESULTS?

Take a few moments to examine the overall ratings.

- If you have all '+1', keep up the good work.

- If you have a fairly mixed group, you are about average.

- If you have a majority or all '-1', you should seriously consider making changes.

HELP, I'M SURROUNDED BY NEGATIVE PEOPLE.

You can make some changes in one of two ways:

- Replace the negative people with positive ones. It requires that you consciously surround yourself with people who have more positive attitudes. Spend less and less time with the negatives. Your time is valuable. **Be selective about who you share your time with.**

- If you work with these people or are related to these negatives, it may be a real challenge to replace them. These people require a different strategy.

You will need to fortify or insulate yourself from the bad attitudes. Mentally prepare yourself before being with them. Use the strategies discussed earlier such as mental prayer requesting that you be surrounded by a shield or visualize yourself protected by a protective bubble. Maybe they will start to recognize those changes in your attitude.

Surrounding yourself with positive people and insulating your self from negative people will go a long way toward improving your own attitude. Besides: Being around positive, life-giving people is a lot more fun!

Chapter 4
SPEAK UP

The words 'I am...' are potent words.
-A.L. Kitselman

The entire quote from Kitselman reads, "The words 'I am...' are potent words; be careful what you hitch them to. The thing you are claiming has a way of reaching back and claiming you." When it comes to staying positive, what we say to ourselves can make all of the difference in the world. Saying the 'right' things to ourselves is often a real challenge for most of us. The mental self-talk can often be very subtle and therefore challenging to change. But it can be changed and must be changed in order to become more positive. You can achieve amazing results with just a few simple changes.

THE POWER OF AFFIRMATIONS

One way to begin this change is to create affirmations for ourselves. Affirmations should be said out loud and need to be repeated frequently. It has been my experience that repeating your affirmations out loud will be much more beneficial because we are involving more senses into the experience.

This isn't a real surprise, just reiterates some general principles from education. While teaching, for a time I worked with hearing impaired students. Early on, I learned that I needed to get the information to all of my students in as many sensory formats as possible. Some people are visual learners, some tactile and others were primarily auditory. Most students would sit in on a lecture, they would see the illustrations utilized in the lecture in addition to the overhead notes that I would write down on the overhead projector or blackboard. Most students would also hear the lecture material and then write down key words and phrases in their notes. On average most students received the information on three channels: auditory, visual, and kinesthetic. The majority of us have a preference for one of these but we still receive input from all three.

In general, my hearing impaired students were accompanied to class by an interpreter and note taker. So these students watched the interpreter instead of the professor and illustrations. They also did not take in the information kinesthetically by writing notes for themselves. They were from the start receiving information in two less senses than the rest of the students. This presented some unique challenges and opportunities to the instructors and students.

By keeping this in mind when we put our affirmations together, we need to integrate as many senses as possible into both creating and incorporating them into our thoughts. We make them tactile by writing them out over and over again. We make them audible by listening to ourselves saying them out loud or by recording them and playing them repeatedly. We make them visible by posting them someplace where we can view them regularly, places like the bathroom mirror or dashboard of a car.

HOW TO WRITE AFFIRMATIONS

A lot of information has been compiled as to how affirmations should be put together. These sources all recommend the following basic principles. Affirmations need to be:

- Written and spoken in **Present Tense**:
  I am an organized person.
- Be spoken as a declaration of what you want to achieve not as a denial of what you don't want:

I am my ideal weight (NOT: *I don't want to be fat.*)
- Repeated frequently throughout the day.

Let's take a closer look at these principles. First, **affirmations need to be written and spoken in present tense.** Affirmations need to be stated as if the situation already is a reality for us. Instead of "I will be a great author," it needs to be "I am a great author." This leads to making these affirmations a reality now rather than some unknown date in the future. The "I will..." statement subtly tricks us in to procrastinating or delaying inevitably what we want to take place.

Affirmations need to be spoken as a declaration of what you want to achieve, not as a denial of what you don't want. For most of us it is easier to conceive of the ideas of what we don't want as opposed to want we want. We typically think and tell ourselves, "I don't have enough money to pay my bills; I need to earn more money." We need to replace that mindset of lacking with a mindset of abundance. We need to reprogram our mind with, "I have more than enough money to pay off my bills." Another example would be, "I don't have enough time to finish everything I need to." This needs to be replaced with, "I have enough time to accomplish the things that I choose."

Affirmations need to be repeated frequently throughout the day. This is especially important if we are trying to reprogram our thoughts and approach to life. Many of us play the old ingrained negative tapes in our minds over and over again. By repeating the positive affirmations frequently, we start to replace those old negative tapes with new more positive ones. We need to train our minds to reach for these new positive messages instead of the old negative messages; the only way I know to do that is through time and repetition.

Repetition is especially helpful to break old patterns in stressful times. When things aren't going exactly right, or when we do something embarrassing or make a mistake, the negative self talk comes back.

We bombard our thoughts with, "I wish I hadn't done that" or "how could I be so stupid!" We mentally reinforce the negative thought and focus on it.

If you are having a difficult time writing your own affirmations, there are plenty of great resources available for this. One of my personal favorites is *What To Say When You Talk To Yourself*, by Shad Helmstetter, Ph.D. In this book you can find affirmations for virtually every aspect of your life. For example, if you need an affirmation related to health and exercise, you can find several examples. If you need affirmations to improve your attitude, he has many available. If you want to hone particular skills, such as sales ability or problem solving ability, Dr. Helmstetter has affirmations for these as well.

When I was a child, I can remember my Aunt Virge trying to teach this to me. I would share with her some of the challenges that I was facing; it may have been a school project or scouting badge. Whenever Aunt Virge would hear doubt in my voice or in the words I was saying, she would stop me. She would say, "You know our saying, I CAN DO IT. I want to hear you say it."

Then she would wait for me to say, "I CAN DO IT." Those memories are so vivid and powerful. She was trying to instill in me the tools to make my life what I wanted it to be despite all obstacles. She still does that with me today and will say the same thing to my girls when they are lacking in confidence or express self doubt.

Using affirmations requires us to not only speak the words but to also internalize the words. We need to feel and emotionalize them as well. It is not enough to just say, "I am living debt free," for example. We must visualize in our mind that moment when we pay off all of our outstanding debts. We need to feel how proud and happy we will be at that particular moment.

We need to let that feeling of accomplishment take root inside of us. Repeating your affirmation while internalizing the emotions that go along with the successful completion will make a huge difference in your success.

WHAT TO SAY TO GET THE RESULTS THAT WE WANT.

There is a whole other aspect to Speaking Up. It involves using a positive statement to ask others for the things we want. When my children were young, I attended a class on parenting. At some point in the class, which was geared toward toddlers and pre-school age children, our instructor told us that at this age children can't comprehend contractions. We were told that their brains think in terms of pictures. Therefore, they don't understand the difference between can and can't, don't and do, will and won't, etc.

"Don't eat that" is heard as "eat that." A child's immediate reaction to those instructions is to place whatever is in their hand directly into her mouth. That holds true for "Don't jump on the furniture." "Don't run." And "you can't stick a peanut butter sandwich into the VCR."

When I started to tell my daughters what I wanted, instead of what I didn't want, things changed dramatically. I would say, "Don't jump on the bed" again and again and again until I was screaming with no results. I would say, "You can jump on the floor or sit on the bed." To my surprise, they would actually follow my instructions.

Although this was initially introduced to me as a tool for working with small children, this technique really works well with everyone. People are much more responsive when we ask for what we really want as opposed to asking them to stop what we don't want. How many times do we ask or tell people something using negative language only to get a reaction opposite of our desired results. Saying to a spouse, "let's make plans to go out to dinner every month," will probably get a much better response than "We never go out anymore."

Other examples might be:

1. "I need you here on time for your shift to set a good example for your subordinates."

...as opposed to:

"Don't be late for work again."

2. "It is a good idea for you to take advantage of this opportunity."

...as opposed to:

"You wouldn't want to miss this chance."

3. "I wish you wouldn't do that." Or "Don't do that!"

...as opposed to:

"Next time can you try it this way."

When we consider how our response is to those phrases, we can understand why others respond to us either positively or negatively. Being told what NOT to do often makes us more defensive or more resolved. From experience, when someone tells me what I *can't* do, it generally causes me to dig in my heels and sets my resolve to do it. This type of negative phrasing also lacks the clarity needed to perform the task the way we really want it done.

SPEAK UP Self Talk Quiz

Rate yourself using the following scale.

1 = Never   2 = Rarely
3 = Sometimes   4 = Often
5 = Always

_____ 1. I know my affirmations and repeat them regularly.

_____ 2. I state my requests as positive declarations of what I want. "Arrive to work on time in the future" rather than "Don't be late tomorrow."

_____ 3. When repeating my affirmations, I visualize them as a reality. I see them, feel them, taste them and smell them.

_____ 4. I state my affirmations in Present tense as if they are occurring right now.

_____ 5. When I find myself thinking negative, self-sabotaging thoughts, I replace them with positive self-affirming thoughts.

_____ Total

21-25   **THUMBS UP.** You are really utilizing positive self talk.

16-20   **KEEP IT UP.** You are moving in the right direction.

11-15   **KICK IT UP.** Increase your positive self talk to see some great changes.

5-10   **START UP.** Take the time to incorporate affirmations into your routine.

Chapter 5
LIGHTEN UP

Realize situations change with time. Things that we think are vitally important today may seem insignificant tomorrow.

When we find ourselves in a stressful situation, it is very easy to lose perspective. It is very easy to let things get blown way out of proportion. If we are under stress, what would normally be a small inconvenience takes on gargantuan proportions. If we are in a foul mood, the same is also true. Inconsequential things or events become personal. In our mind, the pot hole in the road finds only our car and causes a flat tire. When we are in a hurry to get someplace, we perceive that every traffic light is red and every driver in front of us is driving too slowly.

THE WORLD ISN'T OUT TO GET YOU; IT JUST FEELS THAT WAY!

For about the first year following our son's death, the slightest thing would set me off in some sort of emotional outburst. I remember seeing a child riding in a car without proper safety restraints; I was so angry that the adults in the car would take this unnecessary risk. Occasionally someone would make an innocent comment about babies or children and I was certain that there was some hidden meaning meant to hurt or anger me.

If I had only lightened up a little, I would have responded so much differently.

If I could have had a little more perspective, these same incidences would have not meant so much. When we find ourselves in highly stressful times, sometimes the only thing we can do is remind ourselves that we are not being singled out by potholes, traffic lights and distracted people who do inconsiderate things.

IS IT REALLY *THAT* IMPORTANT?

The other part of Lighten Up requires us to examine situations and to question the REAL importance of the situation or event. Does this thing that I am making such a big deal out of really matter in the overall scope of life? Will it be of any consequence five years from now? Is it going to impact the quality or value of life for anyone including myself? If the answers are "no," we may just need to let it go.

I can remember getting upset in college over tests and grades. I would lose sleep over a high B in genetics class. I thought my life would end if I wasn't in the top 5% of my class. With the exception of academic institutions, no one has every asked for my GPA on an interview. No one is interested in the fact that that I pulled a B in Russian literature in a summer semester because I was working and also taking calculus and immunology. It doesn't matter to my daughters when I tuck them in at night that I obtained a straight 4.0 in every graduate class that I took.

There is nothing wrong with putting our decisions through a simple test. We need to go back and ask the following questions:

- Does this really matter in the overall scope of life?
- Will it be of any consequence five years from now?
- Is it going to impact the quality or value of life for anyone (including myself)?
- Will I look back on this and regret taking or not taking action?

PHYSICAL SURROUNDINGS.

Lightening Up involves your physical surroundings as well. I am constantly amazed by how many advertisements and Do It Yourself shows are dedicated to this. There are whole businesses dedicated to organizing closets, offices, and rooms. One show brings a scale to the home and actually weighs the items that are removed from the home in the form of trash and charitable donations! You can purchase bags to shrink down the "stuff" to take up less space. You can find storage containers in every size and color. People rent and keep items in long term storage areas for years.

One result of modern society is that we just have much more 'stuff'. I know that I fall prey to this. We were planning to go camping this past summer with my extended family. When getting ready for the trip, I remember discussing with my husband which tent to take. We love camping and backpacking so we had several choices. We had the new backpacking tent that all four of us could sleep in; we had the old backpacking tent comfortable for my husband and me, but uncomfortable with the girls and our dog. We could also select from the extra large family tent with attached screen room that is affectionately known as the 'condo'. We also have a midsize tent, tall enough for my husband to stand in. I actually started to laugh; I could not believe that we had accumulated so many different tents over the last several years.

I started to think of all of the duplicate things that we own. Things were duplicated for a variety of reasons. We had two infant car seats. Now we have four boosters, two for each car. I am sure we could get by with two, but now I don't have to transfer seats prior to trips.

I couldn't even count how many biology text books I own. Every year new additions were available, and of course, different colleges used different texts. So I had two to three different texts each semester. Each of these had different laboratory manuals as well and also a teacher's guide to go with them.

I am not an expert by any means on organization. (I am still working on it. One of my affirmations is: *I am an organized person.*) But I am sure that eliminating the clutter that surrounds me and my family would make life a lot simpler, thereby removing a great deal of stress and frustration that goes into searching for missing items.

I was discussing this very topic with a colleague. She has a new rule of thumb that helps her determine what stays and what goes from her home. I love it; her rule is so easy: If it is not something that serves a benefit to getting the family to their goals, or if it does not represent a personal or family value, then the item goes. For example, if you value quality time together as a family, the family vacation photos can stay. Another friend has the rule that for every new item that comes into her home, at least one no-longer-useful item needs to go out.

These two ideas can take you a long way to really lightening up your physical surroundings. Ask the questions, "Will this be of any consequence five years from now? Is it going to impact the quality or value of life for anyone including myself?" The answers will let you know if you need to lighten up emotionally as well. Most of us will feel a lot better if we 'lighten up'.

Chapter 6
LISTEN UP

Garbage in = Garbage out.

Just before the birth of our first daughter, I took on a position in sales. The particular company is very well known for its outstanding sales training. Early on in the training one of our instructors shared with us a very important piece of advice. She said, "GARBAGE IN EQUALS GARGAGE OUT." She was attempting to convey to us the importance of what we read and listen to. She encouraged us to be very selective about what we listen to on the radio and watch on television. We should also be careful about what we choose to read.

For most of my life, I was very involved in a great many activities and watching the evening news broadcasts and television in general was just something that did not fit into my daily routine. In my mid 20s, there was a time period when I was living alone. I would eat dinner with the local and network news as company. And then again at 11pm, I would watch the news before turning in to bed. In the morning I would have a news show on while eating breakfast and getting ready for work. I knew all of the news that was taking place in Detroit, in the nation and in the world.

The television shows that I watched, which were a lot at the time, weren't of the best quality either. I am not quite sure when, but at some point I realized that this was taking a toll on me. It started to affect me in some not-so-positive ways. I began to feel helpless; like I had no impact on the things that were happening in the world.

Why should I bother trying when there are so many--too many--screwed up people out there? I could go to work each day, help my family, work to improve my community and still feel helpless. I was feeling more and more isolated instead of more and more connected to the world.

At some point, I stopped watching the news and became more selective of the shows that I watched. Even without watching the news it is amazing how much you can learn from the radio, conversations with colleagues, and catching glimpses of the headline features. The internet also makes it easy to stay on top of current events.

It took some time, but eventually my outlook on life began to improve. I was no longer helpless. I began to feel like I could once again impact the world around me.

The motivating force for most broadcast media is profit. Advertisers place ads where people will see them. And face it, sensational stories typically attract larger audiences; the news media provides what the audience wants.

As a nation, we witnessed the full impact of this on September 11, 2001. I was at home taking care of our two-year-old daughter when the first plane hit the World Trade Center. We had the television on that morning when the local broadcast was interrupted. When the second plane hit, I, like the rest of the nation that witnessed it, knew that we were at war.

Because our children were so young at the time, my husband, John, and I really felt a need to protect them from the events that were taking place. We explained what was happening and kept the television turned off. We got most of our information from the radio and from the television after our children went to bed. We tried our best to keep our daily routines as intact as possible.

I remember reading an article a few weeks later about the impact of the constant exposure to the images. It talked about how it was impacting people and inducing feelings of anger and helplessness. It addressed how the feelings and emotions were elicited time and time again as the people watched replay after replay. It was also suggested that this was particularly unhealthy for small children who didn't yet have the proper under-standing of the concept of time. How each time they viewed a replay, to them it was actually as if the original crash was taking place again.

It wasn't until that point that I realized how we had started out trying to protect our children but ultimately helped ourselves out. I am not saying that it is okay to close our eyes to the injustices that are taking place around us. We just need to be careful about how we are taking in this information and about how we are letting it impact what actions we take in response. If we take in the information and allow it to incapacitate us, that is not right or healthy. We need to be able to take in the information that will spur us to pro-action.

The whole point of this is that we need to be very careful of what we listen to. We need to be very selective of the music that we choose and the news information that we watch and listen to. Those sources also need to be credible sources that are not solely bent on sensationalizing. Good, credible resources are available.

The majority of people in the news industry are reputable. They work in a highly pressured environment where being first matters a great deal; being accurate is just as important. They are generally highly motivated people who aren't interested in exploitation. Like in other professions, they endure the reputation of unscrupulous, sensationalizing colleagues.

SOME ALTERNATIVES.

So where do you find less negative sources for new and information? How can you keep abreast of what is going on without being brought down? This isn't always so easy but it is possible.

- One way is to limit the amount of news coverage you watch.

- Another option might be to just listen to the news as opposed to watching the news. There are times when we really need to SEE the images of what is going on to absorb the full impact. It would be very hard to understand the impact of September 11 on New York City without the photos and video footage. It is very difficult to fully comprehend the devastation to Louisiana and Mississippi by Hurricanes Katrina and Rita without seeing the images. But for the everyday, general news, I find that just listening to the broadcast is sufficient. It is possible to listen to the television while preparing dinner, doing laundry or other tasks. This way, you can hear what is going on in the world without viewing the images.

- Another option might be to get your information from radio broadcasts. I spend a lot of time in the car these days, driving back and forth to school and other activities. This car time is used to catch glimpses of what is going on in my local area and also globally.

- I especially feel fortunate to live in an area so close to the U.S./Canadian border. This way I can listen to some of the news from Canada to get a completely different perspective on events. Today it is easier than ever to listen to news reports from a variety of countries.

- I would caution that, just like with television broadcasts, you need to be selective in which radio stations you choose to listen to. Different broadcasters, journalists and radio show hosts definitely color the news, well, differently. I can think of two morning radio show hosts in our area who always follow just about every news piece with a negative commentary. They are constantly pointing out problems and complaining, in contrast to another local broadcaster that is always searching for solutions.

- A quick trip to the internet should lead you to some additional sources that are less negative and more proactive or solution oriented.

- You can even find some shows that are much more positive listed under Positive News on the internet. I was amazed when I first started searching for the variety that is available.

- Another great thing to do is to use our listening time for listening to audible books or motivational information. I attend a monthly meeting that will keep me in my car for about three hours (1.5 hours each way). I love listening to audible books while driving; it is amazing how fast the trip is when I am engaged in a great book or listening to a great speaker. There are unlimited sources available for this. A trip to a local library can provide some of this material; many communities have books-on-tape stores for visually impaired individuals. You can also subscribe to internet providers for downloading books, for example, *www.audible.com*. More and more authors are now offering their books in audible forms, and your local bookstore or *www.Amazon.com* can help you locate them.

WHAT ABOUT LISTENING TO MUSIC?

The music we listen to can really impact us as well. Listening to songs that were popular at different times in my life can bring back memories very vividly. I can remember listening to some sad ballads after breaking up with my first boyfriend. I was heartbroken; if I hear those songs, it still elicits memories from that time. Just like hearing other songs reminds me of the fun of living in a small college dormitory or of when my husband and I were newlyweds.

All of us have probably heard the old joke about Country-Western music; play it backwards and you get your dog back, your truck back and your wife back. Personal experience has taught me that the music I listen to can profoundly affect my moods. I am sure most of us can think of songs that elicit strong responses, both mental and physical. Now before a speaking engagement, I listen to a couple of my favorite songs by *Great Big Sea*. After doing so, my whole body feels fully alive and ready to move with enthusiasm and vigor.

In my personal experience, music is similar to the chicken and the egg. Which came first? At times we select songs to listen to because of the mood we are in. Other times we hear a song and as a result we conjure up memories and feelings.

My older daughter, Jacquelyn, even commented about one of her favorite songs one morning. We were listening to the song on the radio while driving. "Mom, dad," she asked, "why doesn't she just stop listening to it?"

I thought, "What are you talking about? Why doesn't *who* stop *what*?"

"What, honey?" I replied.

Jacquelyn was referring to the artist performing the song that was playing in our car right then. "She (the artist) said in the song that she feels her heart breaking every time she hears the song..... So why doesn't she just stop listening to it?" Jacky said back to me.

Wow, out of the mouths of babes.

Chapter 7
CHANGE UP

The wisest person is not the one who has the fewest failures, but the one who turns failures to best account.
-Richard Grant

Change Up refers to our ability to change the way we view the events of our life. This is sometimes referred to as 'reframing' a situation or event. It means that you take the negative events and try to shine a whole new perspective on them. This may mean trying to find the positive out of a difficult situation or simply putting it into perspective.

This particular step requires us to make a choice. We must choose to either focus on the negative, or seek out the positive when faced with a challenging situation. There are steps we can take to make this choice easier. If we choose to seek out the positive in the small difficulties that we face, it starts to become a habit; it really does start to become a habit to start looking for the best. Then when we face a true crisis, it is easier to search out the positive outcomes.

Everyone one of us face challenges and disappointments; the real key is what we do with those disappointments. Thomas Edison lost his lab in West Orange to a fire in 1914. Because the lab was considered fireproof, it was drastically underinsured and insurance would not come close to cover the cost of rebuilding. The amazing thing was Edison's response to this disaster. Rather than being devastated by the loss, he viewed the fire as a way to get rid of old mistakes and rubbish. Three weeks later, he had a considerable portion of his facility back up and running.

There will be times in life when we do face a crisis or truly unfortunate event. Positive people search for the positive outcomes from these events. It sometimes may take years to find those outcomes, but people with a positive outlook are confident that they will recognize it when it finally occurs.

The Walsh family lived a parent's worst nightmare when their son, Adam, was kidnapped. As a result, the Walsh family was the catalyst for many things to prevent others from experiencing this horror. When Adam was abducted, I am sure that his parents could never see what good could come from such a tragedy. In no small part due to his parents' diligence, the loss of Adam has led to changes that have saved so many other parents from experiencing the loss of their children.

Tragic losses have led to innumerable benefits to all; they have led to stalking laws, domestic violence shelters, child safety caps, seat belts, air bags, improved medications and medical treatments. All of these things were developed to be a positive outcome from sad or negative situations.

All of us will face a crisis or problem at some point in time. We then have to make a choice. We have to choose to view something as a 'problem' or an 'inconvenience'. We need to decide if we are going to remain the victim of a tragedy or whether we are going to rise above the situation and find the positive-ness which can only come from that tragedy.

Chapter 8
LIFT UP

We cannot hold a torch to light another's path without brightening our own.
-Ben Sweetland

Sometimes a really simple way to feel better is to help someone else. First off this can get your mind thinking about something other than your own situation.

Second, it allows you to feel that your efforts have a positive impact. Third, it helps you put your own problems into a new perspective. **The true way to soften one's troubles is to solace those of others.** **-Madame de Maintenon**

It is very easy to let the difficulties and challenges we face to consume our thoughts. We spend our time and energy focusing on what is wrong. We worry or obsess over the problems we have.

SWITCH THE FOCUS AWAY FROM YOUR OWN STRUGGLES.

When we help someone else, we need to take our mind and change what it is focusing on. When we are engaged in helping another person, we take the focus off of our wants and needs to focus on their wants and needs. If we are working on a way to help someone else, we aren't worrying about ourselves. We need to step out of our own situation, at least temporarily, in order to focus in on the needs of others.

From experience, it is pretty hard to have a bad day and deliver food to 'shut ins'; the gratitude of the seniors brightens your day. You can't help but feel better when you read to a book to a group of four year olds who need a positive role model in their life. You might feel exhausted, but you feel great after spending the day building a Habitat for Humanity home side by side with the future owner.

YOUR ACTIONS REALLY DO MAKE A DIFFERENCE.

When we help others, it also gives us the sense of impact on the world. When working in campus ministry, we dealt with this issue a great deal. Many students, at this critical point in life, didn't understand or realize the impact of their activities on the world. They often felt that since they couldn't impact everyone, why try to impact anyone? Many felt helpless or had a why-bother attitude. The world they were growing up in often perpetuated this philosophy. They were leading egocentric lives, focusing on their own education, social life, and friends. They weren't earning enough income to support someone else; they weren't raising small children; they weren't making a major societal impact in their work. They often didn't see themselves as contributing to the society as a whole.

It was so thrilling for me to join them on spring break opportunities. We would leave our local suburban community and travel hundreds of miles to live and work in rural communities. They would learn some basic building skills and work with homeowners to renovate and update homes. I was truly amazed at the end of a week's time to see how much they accomplished. We would videotape them at the end of the week at the individual sites, showcasing, with a great deal of pride, the work they had done. Several weeks later we would gather together for a reunion. Year after year, the students talked about how their lives were forever changed by these experiences. Often for the first time in their lives, they experienced a real sense of accomplishment and saw how their actions impacted other human beings.

PUT YOUR PROBLEMS INTO A NEW PERSPECTIVE.

A third benefit to helping other people is that it allows us to put our own challenges and difficulties into a whole new perspective. It is hard to feel sorry for yourself because you can't afford to buy that new CD player when you have just spent a week helping someone who couldn't afford to put a roof on their house. I'm not saying this gives you permission to pity others, but it gives you the ability to feel compassion for others. It often makes you feel very fortunate for the blessings that you do have.

Someone once said if given the opportunity we would all select our own challenges as opposed to the challenges faced by other people. Imagine a whole group of people gathered into a circle. Everyone is required to throw into the circle their problems. Everyone is then required to retrieve problems from the center. As the individuals stand at the outside of the circle looking into the pile of problems that everyone else was facing, each gladly reaches into that pile and slowly takes back their own problems.

Chapter 9
CHARGE UP

Small victories will lead to larger victories by changing our view of our own personal success and ability.

This past summer, my oldest daughter learned how to ride a bicycle. While she was learning how to ride a bicycle I was learning about life. This whole process took quite a long time because we live on a very busy street without sidewalks. This goal was put on our family Yearly Goal Poster last year. When we didn't complete that goal, we put it on this year's as well. The speed limit on our street is 45mph. This made it difficult to practice bike riding. If we wanted to ride, we would either have to load the bikes into our van and drive to the park or walk the bikes to area in the neighborhood with sidewalks.

While learning, we tried both options repeatedly. I thought this was going to be easy for me; after all, I have spent the majority of my adult life educating people. I will admit that teaching your own children is very different than teaching adults! We experienced a great deal of frustration, both Jacky and I. Tears were shed, she was afraid of falling when I let go. Having cars whiz past at 45-50 mph was also intimidating. She was embarrassed because she couldn't ride as well as some of the other kids at school. I thought the activities that we were trying were building up her confidence, but in reality they were not.

August had arrived in Michigan. The school year was going to begin and once more I felt like I was letting Jacky down by not teaching her to ride. I decided that I was just going to pick a day that she was going to learn and let her know that was the day and put it on our calendar. I contacted my sister and asked if she wanted to go to Metro Beach with me to help with the kids. Mari and I planned everything out. She would work with my nephew, Alex, and my younger daughter, Kylee. This would free me up to help Jacky.

Jacky knew that morning that we were going to the park to learn to ride a bicycle. We loaded up in the car, brought along some water and I put on my running shoes to keep up with her. This attempt (unlike our other attempts) worked.

What was different? Jacky was surrounded by a group of cheerleaders, Alex, Kylee and Aunt Mari Jo. Another difference was the atmosphere. We had a nicely paved walkway that went out to the end of a point extending into Lake Saint Clair, no cars rushing by to make her (or mom) nervous.

The most important difference was that we created a lot of small victories for Jacky. First she had to ride with me just holding on to the handle bars, where I gradually let her take over more control of steering the bicycle. When we did that for a while, we stopped and celebrated with water at a pretty garden spot. Then we went around the park again, this time she would tell me when I could let go of the handlebars. Aunt Mari Jo faithfully counted how many seconds she rode unassisted. When she fell over or put her feet down to stop, Aunt Mari Jo would yell out, "13 seconds." We would all cheer. Next she yelled "28 seconds.......55 seconds.......63.......77......105 seconds!"

Before I knew it, she was riding on her own and was building up her self confidence with each try. Soon we were setting goals by distance, "Okay Jacky," I would say, "ride from here to the two trees....Now ride to the pavilion." We eventually made our way back to the concession stand and celebrated with ice cream. All the while Jacky was basking in the admiration of her little sister and younger cousin.

Jacky went to the park with the determination to learn to ride. She started out accomplishing small goals which eventually grew bigger and bigger until she successfully completed what she set out to achieve. This was by far the most successful and least stressful experience for all of us.

As adults, we sometimes set audacious goals. This is great, we need that in order to dream and think big. We need the big goals so that we can set the course. We need to be able to see where we want to be, even if it is well past the horizon. What we sometimes forget to do, however, is to set the plan or strategy to get to the ultimate destination. Without this we lose steam and set ourselves up for failure. We then beat ourselves up because we didn't make it to our final destination.

For example, we set a goal to lose 50 pounds. We begin a starvation diet, exercise until we collapse, and jump on a scale every half hour. Then at the end of the first week we have lost five pounds. Because we get to the end of the second week and have only lost two more pounds, we convince ourselves that we are failures (great self-talk) and we quit. We eat an entire pizza or ½ gallon of Rocky Road ice cream to comfort our injured egos and quit exercising and eating healthy.

When we set that big huge audacious goal, we need to give our selves plenty of small victories along the way. We need to celebrate the fact that we made it through that first meal without overindulging. We need to pat ourselves on the back when we take that flight of stairs to the third floor instead of the elevator. We need to reward ourselves when we make better choices at the "grazing table" at the company after-work mixer. We need to celebrate the two pounds that we lost at the end of the week! We need to set ourselves up with small victories for it is the small victories that will ultimately take us to our final goal.

So let's say your goal is to have a more positive attitude. Instead of expecting to wake up each day ready to take on whatever life sends our way (especially if getting out of bed in the morning is a struggle) set a realistic goal of repeating affirmations in the shower. The next day, go out of your way to do something to lift up another person. Each day add one more thing to improve your attitude. Celebrate the small victories along the way; make sure you celebrate after you leave the family get-together where you successfully let all the negative, 'well-intentioned', comments roll off your back. Cheer when you find yourself smiling while stuck in a traffic jam. Make sure you recognize and celebrate the day when you realize that you finally have developed the habit of being positive!

Chapter 10
REACH UP

It is faith that breathes life into hope. It is hope that fuels a positive life-giving attitude.

When I think of all of the people that I admire most for their consistently positive attitude, the one common denominator that I find is hope. The source of this hope is their spirituality. All of these people have a deep spirituality that they can tap into when they have exhausted their own internal resources.

All of them define spirituality differently. Their spirituality can be centered around God, Allah, The Great Spirit, Inner Guide or Inner Source to name a few. But it is always present. All have a deeply connected or personal relationship with their spirituality. The paths are different. The common denominator is hope that is born of faith.

Those people who day in and day out exhibit a life giving attitude all have some spiritual resource in their life to pull from. They know that ultimately there is a greater reserve that they can tap into when experiencing difficult times. **It is faith that breathes life into hope. It is hope that fuels a positive life giving attitude.**

Those who don't acknowledge their spirituality generally do it out of a fear of having to relinquish control over their circumstances. When we relinquish control we view ourselves as less self-sufficient. We live in a society that values self-sufficiency and individualism. We fear not being self-sufficient; we fear growing older and losing our driver's license and our independence. We somehow equate dependence with value; if you are more dependent on others, you are less valuable. You had better not reach a point where you can't take care of yourself.

While staying home to raise our daughters, I struggled a lot with these issues. For the first time in my adult life, I was financially dependent on someone else and it did not sit well with me. I deemed myself less valuable because I was not earning a living, completely ignoring that fact that I was doing the important job of raising our family. I am sure that if you ask anyone who has, out of their own choice or not, relinquished their independence, they would also share how they felt less worthy or less valuable.

I find it is ironic when people relinquish control over to the Spiritual Force in their life only to find that they have more confidence as opposed to less confidence. When we acknowledge that we are not completely independent from our Spiritual Center, a major change takes place; it is by giving up control that they actually gain control.

For me, the spiritual source is God. I can honestly say that in my own personal experiences it was faith alone that pulled me through the tough times. It was due to faith that I didn't come out from painful experiences embittered and jaded. It was faith that allowed me to step out into the unknown with a confidence that things would get better. It was, and still is, faith which gives me the confidence to know that no matter what the future brings, I will be able to access something greater than myself and my own limited resources. I am confident that God will supply me with the things I truly need, the people who can truly help me, the inner strength to persist through.

I know that...

It is faith that breathes life into hope. It is hope that fuels a positive life-giving attitude.

Chapter 11
NEVER, EVER, EVER, EVER GIVE UP

We conquer by continuing.
-George Matheson

No matter how positive of a person you are we all have tough days. We all have those mornings when we wake up in a bad mood, or days when we are struggling with the situation we find ourselves in. These are the times when we need to remember it is okay to start once again in taking steps to stay positive. These are the times when we need to pick up those affirmations that we haven't said in awhile. We need to make time to call a friend who has a positive attitude. *In order to live it up, we must never ever, ever, ever give up.*

We need to remember that attitude is a choice. We really can make it a habit to have a positive attitude. We need to re-examine to see if we are lifting up others, if we are changing up the events of our lives, if we are reaching up to connect with our spiritual source.

In addition to never giving up on cultivating a positive attitude, we must never give up on our dreams. These dreams give us hope; they reveal the greatness that exists within each of us. All too often we settle for good when great is just around the corner. Frequently people give up just before the race is finally won; just before the dream becomes a reality.

At a meeting I recently attended, a colleague reminded me of a quote from

Winston Churchill. After researching the quote I found that it came from a speech that Churchill gave at Harrow School in 1941. This quote fit so appropriately in this chapter that I had to include it.

> Never give in – never, never, never, never, in nothing great or small, large or petty, never give in except to convictions of honour and good sense. Never yield to force; never yield to the apparently overwhelming might of the enemy.
>
> Sir Winston Churchill

For many of us, that "apparently overwhelming...enemy" is staring back at us from the mirror each morning. By continuously 'settling' for less than our dreams, we become that enemy to our own success. We are the ones who sabotage our own happiness and fulfillment. In her book, *A Return To Love: Reflections on the Principles of A Course in Miracles*, Marianne Williamson reminds us of the source of our self sabotaging behavior.

Our Deepest Fear

Our deepest fear is not that we are inadequate. Our deepest fear is that we are powerful beyond measure. It is our light, not our darkness that most frightens us.

We ask ourselves, Who am I to be brilliant, gorgeous, talented, fabulous? Actually, who are you not to be?
You are a child of God.

Your playing small does not serve the world. There is nothing enlightened about shrinking so that other people won't feel insecure around you. We are all meant to shine, as children do.

We were born to make manifest the glory of God that is within us. It is not just in some of us; it is in everyone.

And as we let our own light shine, we unconsciously give other people permission to do the same. As we are liberated from our own fear, our presence automatically liberates others.

(Marianne Williamson, A Return To Love: Reflections on the Principles of a Course in Miracles, Harper Collins, 1992. From Chapter 7, Section 3)

Do you want to remain a slave to your fears? What are you willing to give up on? Are you willing to let go of your dreams? Are you willing to live a life of mediocrity instead of the life that you were created for? By living this life of mediocrity, who besides yourself are you letting down? Who is going to learn from your example? Are you willing to let those who are watching you, including your children, grow up to be quitters?

Go ahead. Make the decision today to have a more positive attitude. ***In order to live it up, we must never ever, ever, ever give up.***

Chapter 12
KEEP IT UP

Now that you have determined what you need to do to improve and maintain your positive attitude, its time to set up a plan of action. Without a plan it will be difficult to carry out your intentions. A plan will help you make having a more positive attitude a reality.

Let's take a look at the previous chapters. Take some time to review what you want to accomplish from each chapter; what are your own personal goals as it relates to each topic? After taking time to reflect on our goals, we can then establish a plan of action. Keep in mind that old saying, "How do you eat an elephant?" Answer: One bite at a time!

In Chapter 1 we examined the reasons for, and benefits of, having a positive attitude. Take a few minutes to reflect on your reasons for improving your attitude. Is it to improve your health? Do you want to improve your leadership ability? Is it your plan to positively impact the young people in your life? Maybe you just want to enjoy life more.

Take a few minutes to reflect on your own personal reasons for reading this book and for improving your attitude; jot down some notes. When you have a clear purpose in mind it will make it easier to stay focused on your goals.

_____

_____

_____

_____

_____

_____

_____

In Chapter 2, Wake Up, we learned that we are all personally responsible for our own happiness. Other people can't make us happy. Take some time to reflect on this. Do we relinquish the control for our attitude to others? Are we postponing our happiness by waiting for the 'If onlys' in life. "If only I had a better job. If only I had a better spouse." Have we reached a point where we recognize that we can choose to be positive? Do we choose how we react to situations? Are we proactive or reactive?

Who do I relinquish control of my happiness to?

_____

_____

_____

_____

In what ways do I postpone my personal happiness?

_____

_____

_____

_____

Am I ready to make the decision to take control of my attitude? Why or why not?

_____
_____
_____
_____

In Chapter 3, Link Up, we took a look at the relationships we have with others. We evaluated the relationships we have with the people closest to us to determine if they have a positive of negative effect. We also discussed some strategies for dealing with people with negative attitudes.

As a result of evaluating my relationships, I discovered:

_____
_____
_____
_____

Chapter 4, Speak Up, required us to look at the language we use. It explored the use of affirmations and positive declarations. What we say has truly a powerful effect on our attitude and results.

These are my affirmations.

_____

_____

_____

_____

_____

_____

_____

_____

_____

_____

_____

_____

_____

_____

_____

_____

_____

In Lighten Up we focused on determining what is truly most important to our lives and our happiness. Things that we take so seriously will often lose importance as time passes. We need to assess if we are focusing too much energy on things that in the long run really will not matter.

What things do I need to 'Lighten Up' about?

_____

_____

_____

_____

When we have chosen to have a more positive approach to live, we then need to examine the things that we listen to. We need to make sure that the television shows, music and radio programs, and other media we expose ourselves to be consistent with what we want for our life. Remember, GARBAGE IN = GARBAGE OUT.

What adjustments do I need to make in terms of my selections for television, music, and news sources?

_____

_____

_____

_____

In Chapter 7, Change Up, we discussed the importance of taking the difficult things that we have experienced and changing how we view them. We saw how successful people like Thomas Edison took tragedies and turned them into triumphs. Even the little irritations, such as traffic jams and long lines, provide us with opportunities to practice this skill.

What is my normal response to daily inconveniences or irritations?

_____

_____

_____

_____

Is there a major event that has occurred in my life that I have yet to view as an opportunity? What 'good' things resulted or can potentially result from this event?

_____

_____

_____

_____

_____

_____

_____

_____

What do I need to work on to find the positive outcomes from this event?

_____

_____

_____

_____

One very effective way to improve attitude involves helping other people. In Chapter 8, Lift Up, we discussed how community service or simple acts of charity can really improve our attitude. It let us see that we are actually having a positive influence on others as well as allowing us to forget about our own problems and concerns for a short period of time.

Describe how you felt after performing an act to lift up another person or group of people?

_____

_____

_____

_____

What talents do I have that I can share through community service?

_____

_____

_____

_____

In Charge Up, we focused on creating small victories in order to lead to larger victories. We saw how that the small steps, or the small wins, accumulate and build our self esteem.

What are the small victories that I can start creating for myself right now?

_____

_____

_____

_____

We also examined the importance of connecting to our spirituality in Chapter 10, Reach Up. Hope results from having that spiritual connection. All of us need to have a spiritual source to tap into when we have exhausted our own personal resources.

Can I recall an experience where my spiritual source provided me with faith to get through a difficult situation? Describe that experience.

_____

_____

_____

_____

_____

_____

_____

_____

What am I currently doing to develop my spirituality?

_____

_____

_____

_____

Now that we have taken time to review the things that will lead us to a more positive outlook on life, we need to put this information into action. It is time to *become pro-active* instead of *reactive*. We need to put an action plan into motion.

For most of us, trying to change our outlook can appear daunting—like the analogy of eating an elephant; and like the analogy, even the most daunting tasks can be accomplished if taken one step at a time. The elephant can be eaten, but it must be done one bite at a time.

Repetition is the key to developing a habit. We can develop the habit of having a more positive outlook. Many studies show that it takes 21 days of repetition for an activity to become a habit. For example, starting every morning with affirmations, prayer or meditation can become a daily habit if we first do it for 21 days without interruption. With this premise in mind, we are going to pick one or two activities to do for the next 21 days.

Take a look at the various chapters. Determine an activity that you can do for each chapter. Some examples would include writing and saying your affirmations, or dedicating daily time to prayer/meditation to improve your spiritual life. After you have done this, you will choose the first couple of activities to concentrate on for the next 21 days. Take some time to complete your 21 DAY ACTION PLAN. Do it today before you become distracted.

---

21 DAY ACTION PLAN

WAKE UP   _____
           _____
           _____

LINK UP   _____
           _____
           _____

SPEAK UP   _____
           _____
           _____

LIGHTEN UP   _____
           _____
           _____

LISTEN UP _____
_____
_____

CHARGE UP _____
_____
_____

LIFT UP _____
_____
_____

CHARGE UP _____
_____
_____

REACH UP _____
_____
_____

FOR THE NEXT 21 DAYS, I PLAN ON
IMPLEMENTING THE FOLLOWING ACTIVITIES
(Select 1-3 activities from your list above.)

_____
_____
_____
_____

Start Date: _____

***21 Days Later: _____

*** Mark this date on your calendar***

At the end of the 21 days, take some time to evaluate your progress. Reflect on the activities that have worked very well for you. Have you begun to notice changes in your attitude? What things were more challenging? Do you need to keep working on these? What has been your biggest success? What has been your biggest challenge? What are you going to implement in the next 21 days?

FOR THE NEXT 21 DAYS, I PLAN ON IMPLEMENTING THE FOLLOWING ACTIVITIES (Select 1-3 activities):

_____

_____

_____

_____

_____

Start Date: _____

***21 Days Later: _____

*** Mark this date on your calendar***

Once again take some time to reflect on your progress. Are you recognizing changes in your attitude? Have people started to notice a difference in your attitude? Make sure you spend some time choosing those things that you want to continue working on for the next 21 days.

FOR THE NEXT 21 DAYS, I PLAN ON IMPLEMENTING THE FOLLOWING ACTIVITIES (Select 1-3 activities):

_____

_____

_____

_____

_____

Start Date: _____

***21 Days Later: _____

*** Mark this date on your calendar***

This process won't end here. This is a life long journey; and when you need to, take time to review how far you have come. And I can't wait to hear of your successes along the way!

References

**What To Say When You Talk To
Yourself.** Shad Helmstetter, Ph.D.
Pocket Books, 1982.

The Book of Positive Quotations.
Compiled and Arranged by John Cook.
Rubicon Press, Inc. 1993.

**A Return To Love: Reflections on the
Principles of A Course in Miracles,**
Marianne Williamson, Harper Collins,
1992. From Chapter 7, Section 3.

Voyager Group, LLC

presents quality, highly interactive programs,
training events, retreats and keynote addresses on

MOTIVATION and LEADERSHIP.

For more information, or to book Ms. Eubanks to
present at your next event, contact:

**Kathy A. Eubanks
Voyager Group, LLC
51613 Sass Road
Chesterfield, Michigan 48047**

Phone: 586-598-0268

**info@VoyagerGroupLLC.com
www.VoyagerGroupLLC.com
www.KathyEubanks.com**

ORDER FORM

E-MAIL ORDERS to   info@voyagergroupllc.com
                       info@kathyeubanks.com

POSTAL ORDERS to   Voyager Group, LLC
                       51613 Sass Road
                       Chesterfield, MI 48047

ON-LINE ORDERS at www.KathyEubanks.com
                      www.VoyagerGroupLLC.com

Please send me the following books, cd's or e-books.
_____
_____

Please send more FREE information on:
☐ Other Books   ☐ Audio books   ☐ Speaking/Training
Please e-mail information to me on new products and upcoming events.
E-mail: _____

Name: _____
Address: _____
_____
City, State, Zip: _____
Telephone: _____

Sales Tax: Please include appropriate sales tax. State of Michigan: 6%. California: 7.75%.

Shipping: Please see website for appropriate fees.
www.KathyEubanks.com

Payment: __ Cheque   __ Credit Card __ MO
__ Visa   __ MC   __ Amex
Card number: _____
Name on Card: _____
Exp. Date: _____ Zip: _____